NON-VIOLENCE IS

NOT AN EASY THING

TO UNDERSTAND,

...s be,

...L LESS TO

...d steer

...CTISE, WEAK AS

...ter sea,

...RE, WE MUST

...e Future's portal

ACT PRAYERFULLY

With the Past's blood-rusted key.

AND HUMBLY AND

- James Russell Lowell

CONTINUALLY ASK

GOD TO OPEN THE

EYES OF OUR

UNDERSTANDING,

...eace.

BEING EVER READY

TO ACT ACCORDING

...ime, o Lord!

TO THE LIGHT AS WE

Book of Common Prayer

RECEIVE IT. M K Gandhi

Don't tell me Peace has broken out?
Bertolt Brecht, Mother Courage

G000163089

begin in the minds of men,
inds of men that the defences
ust be constructed.

Give Peace a Chance.
Title of Beatles' song

Now the hoes, the hard mattocks

and beaked plough share the

wealth of the countryside! Let

these shine, while weapons grow

dirty with mould. - **Ovid**

They make a wasteland and call it peace.

Calgacus, quoted by Tacitus

First keep the peace within yourself;

then you can also bring peace to others

Thomas a Kempis

THE
BOOK
OF
PEACE

First published in 1997 by
The Appletree Press Ltd, 19-21 Alfred Street,
Belfast BT2 8DL

Tel: +44 (0) 1232 243074
Fax: +44 (0) 1232 246756

The Book of Peace

A catalogue record for this book
is available from The British Library.

ISBN 0-86281-696-3

9 8 7 6 5 4 3 2 1

THE
BOOK
OF
PEACE

A Treasury of Thoughts on Peace

How beautiful upon the mountains are
the feet of him that bringeth good tidings;
that publisheth Peace. ISAIAH, 52:7

When the Moon is in the seventh house
And Jupiter aligns with Mars
Then peace will guide the planets
And love will steer the stars.

Hair (*The Age of Aquarius*)

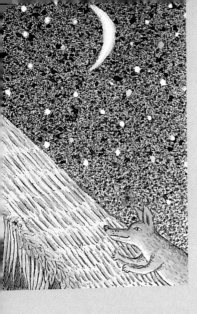

Peace shall steal unaware into our room, and putting her hands across our eyes from behind, shall whisper 'Guess who?' and before we know it, when we least expect it, she is there, to remain by our fireside and bless us and our children with her presence.

LIN YUTANG

Peace – an idea whose time has come
Anatol Rapoport

Nothing can bring you peace but yourself
Ralph Waldo Emerson

Peace and quiet
bring out men's
good qualities

TACITUS

Today we are faced with the pre-eminent fact that if civilisation is to survive, we must cultivate the science of human relationships, the ability of all peoples of all kinds to live together and to work together in the same world at peace.

Franklin D Roosevelt, 1945

What matters all the joy and passion?
Sweet peace, come into my breast!

Johann Wolfgang von Goethe

What is peace? Is it war? No. Is it strife? No.
It is lovely, and gentle, and beautiful;
and pleasant and serene and joyful.

Charles Dickens

Live peacefully with all men.
St Paul, Letter to the Romans

There is enough in the world
for everyone to have plenty to
live on happily and to be at
peace with his neighbours.
Harry S Truman

We ourselves must pilgrims be,
Launch our Mayflower, and steer
Boldly on the desperate winter sea,
Nor attempt the Future's portal
With the Past's blood-rusted key.

- James Russell Lowell

I prefer the most unfair peace
to the most righteous war.

- Marcus Tullius Cicero

I would like to dispose of a part of my fortune to found a prize to be distributed every five or six years... to him or her who has helped... to make the greatest advance towards the idea of general pacification.

Alfred Nobel

Joy is like restless day:
but peace divine
Like quiet night.

Adelaide Anne Procter

If this task of building a peaceful world is the most important of our time, it is also the most difficult. It will, in fact, require far more discipline, more sacrifice, more planning, more thought, more co-operation and more heroism than war ever demanded. - Thomas Merton

Poetry is an act of peace.
Peace goes into the
making of a poet as
flour goes into bread.
PABLO NERUDA

Lord, make me an instrument of your peace:
Where there is hatred, let me sow love,
Where there is injustice, pardon,
Where there is doubt, faith,
Where there is despair, hope,
Where there is dark, light,
Where there is sadness, joy.

St Francis of Assisi

And peace proclaims olives of endless age.

William Shakespeare, *The Rape of Lucrece*

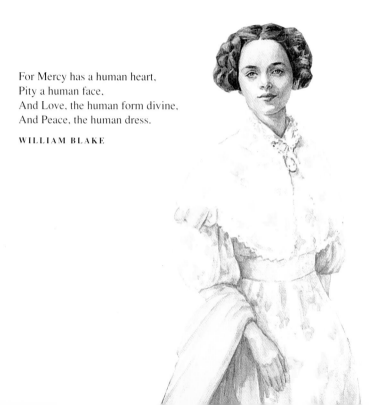

For Mercy has a human heart,
Pity a human face,
And Love, the human form divine,
And Peace, the human dress.

WILLIAM BLAKE

I have desired to go
Where springs not fail,
To fields where flies no sharp and sided hail
And a few lilies blow.

And I have asked to be
Where no storms come,
Where the green swell is in the havens dumb,
And out of the swing of the sea.

GERARD MANLEY HOPKINS

A general definition of civilisation:... the five qualities of truth, beauty, adventure, art, peace.   *Alfred North Whitehead*

Peace is better than war, because in peace sons bury their fathers, while in war, fathers bury their sons.

- Croesus

It is a beauteous evening, calm and free,
The holy time is quiet as a nun,
Breathless with adoration.

William Wordsworth

I conjure up a sweet and peaceful society of brothers, living in eternal concord, all guided by the same principles, all happy in a common happiness, and as my imagination realises a picture so touching, an image of the unattained, I enjoy a momentary taste of true happiness.

JEAN-JACQUES ROUSSEAU

PEOPLE LIKE TRANQUILITY,
AND THEREFORE THEY
LIKE PEACEFUL PRINCES.

Niccolo Macchiavelli

There never was a good war, or a bad peace.

Benjamin Franklin

It's co-existence
Or no existence
- Bertrand Russell

ow the hoes, the hard mattocks

d beaked plough share the

ealth of the countryside! Let

First keep the peace within yourself;

ese shine, while weapons grow

then you can also bring peace to others.

rty with mould. - **Ovid**

Thomas a Kempis

AX

OBISCUM

PEACE BE WITH YOU

ALL THAT TENDS TO UNIFY MANKIND
BELONGS TO THE GOOD AND THE
BEAUTIFUL. ALL THAT TENDS TO
DISUNITE IT IS EVIL AND UGLY.

Leo Tolstoy

LOVE THYSELF LAST, CHERISH THOSE HEARTS
THAT HATE THEE, CORRUPTION WINS NOT
MORE THAN HONESTY, STILL IN THY RIGHT
HAND CARRY GENTLE PEACE.

William Shakespeare, *Henry VIII*

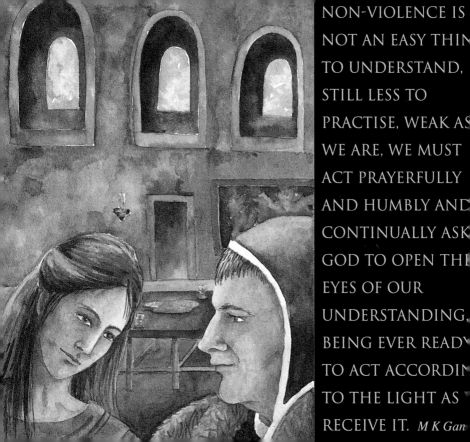

NON-VIOLENCE IS
NOT AN EASY THING
TO UNDERSTAND,
STILL LESS TO
PRACTISE, WEAK AS
WE ARE, WE MUST
ACT PRAYERFULLY
AND HUMBLY AND
CONTINUALLY ASK
GOD TO OPEN THE
EYES OF OUR
UNDERSTANDING,
BEING EVER READY
TO ACT ACCORDING
TO THE LIGHT AS I
RECEIVE IT. *M K Gandhi*

Nation shall speak peace unto nation.

M J Rendall (motto of the BBC)

And while the bubbling and loud-hissing urn
Throws up a steamy column, and the cups
That cheer but not inebriate wait on each,
So let us welcome peaceful evening in.

William Cowper

Observe good faith and justice towards all nations.
Cultivate peace and harmony with all.

George Washington, *Farewell Address*

ANYONE CAN FORGE A LITTLE LINK
OF BROTHERHOOD, OR AT LEAST
UNDERSTANDING. SOME DAY
PERHAPS EVERY BOY AND GIRL
WILL HAVE BECOME AT HOME IN
A FOREIGN COUNTRY, AND THERE
COULD BE NO MORE USEFUL STEP
TOWARDS THE ABOLITION OF WAR.
HAVELOCK ELLIS

Give Peace a Chance.
Title of Beatles' song

Don't tell me Peace has broken out?
Bertolt Brecht, **Mother Courage**

They make a wasteland and call it peace.

Calgacus, quoted by Tacitus

Since wars begin in the minds of men,
it is in the minds of men that the defences
of peace must be constructed.

- UNESCO Constitution

Yes, in the poor man's garden grow
Far more than herbs and flowers;
Kind thoughts, contentment, peace of mind,
And joy for weary hours.
- Mary Howitt

In the ethical progress of man,
mutual support - not mutual
struggle - has had the leading
part. In its wide extension, even
at the present time, we see the
best guarantee of a still loftier
evolution of our race.
- Alexander Kropotkin

THERE WILL COME A TIME WHEN THE WORLD IS INHABITED BY A RACE OF MEN WITH NO FLAW OF FLESH, NO ERROR OF MIND; FREED FROM

NOT ONLY OF DISEASE AND PRIVATION, BUT OF LYING WORDS AND OF LOVE TURNED INTO HATE.

Sarvapalli Radhakhrishnan

Good night, ensured release,
Imperishable peace,
Have these for yours:
While sky and sea and land
And earth's foundations stand
And heaven endures.

- A E Housman

The fact that we, all the human beings now in existence, are the exclusive trustees for carrying any further the progress already achieved by life, is a responsibility which, if sobering, is also inspiring.

- JULIAN HUXLEY

The religion of non-violence is not meant merely for the rishis and saints. It is meant for the common people as well. Non-violence is the law of our species, as violence is the law of the brute.

- M K GANDHI

O my Peace who smilest, thy soft eyes filled with tears,
Summer rainbow, sunny evening;
Who with golden fingers fondlest the besprinkled fields,
Carest for the fallen fruits,
And healest the wounds
Of the trees which the wind and the hail have bruised;
Shed on us thy healing balm
And lull our sorrows to sleep;
They will pass, and we also.
Thou alone endurest for ever.

ROMAIN ROLLAND

He gave his honours t

His blessed part t

- William Shakespeare, *Henry VI*

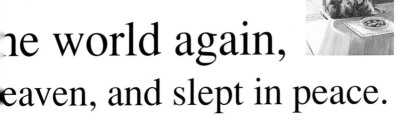

e world again,

eaven, and slept in peace.

The Spirit of Christ, by which we are guided, is not changeable... and will never move us to fight and war against any man with outward weapons, neither for the Kingdom of Christ, nor for the Kingdoms of the world.

George Fox, to King Charles II

All your strength is i
All your damage is i
Therefore be at peac
And like brothers liv

Henry Wadsworth Longfellow, *Hiawatha*

our union,
discord,
enceforward,
ogether.

Lasting peace resides
not in extending the
ties of relationship
among princes by
marriage; nor in
treaties and alliances
which lead to wars...
Men must not be too
zealous about a
phantasm called
national glory, often
inconsistent with
individual happiness.

Erasmus

Come to us, kindly peace!
Bring ears of grain,
and let apples pour forth
from your bright bosom.
Tibullus

Ah! When shall all men's good
Be each man's rule, and universal peace
Be like a shaft of light across the land;
And like a lane of beams athwart the sea,
Through all the circle of the golden year?
Alfred Tennyson

You may either
peace or buy it
by resisting ev
by compromis

win your
win it,
; or buy it,
ng with evil.

Peace has love as its god;
Peace is what we lovers worship.
- Petronius

Peace hath her victories,
No less renowned than War
- John Milton

Give peace in ou

time, o Lord!

Book of Common Prayer

ACKNOWLEDGEMENTS

The publisher wishes to thank the
following artists for illustrations
which appear in *The Book of Peace:*

Jon Berkeley, Laura Cronin,
Colin Davidson, Des Fox,
Clare Hewitt, Milanda Lopez,
Vladimir Lubarov, Joanna Martin,
David McAllister, Ann McDuff,
Andrew Whitson, Cal Williams.

gin in the minds of men,
ds of men that the defences
t be constructed.

Give Peace a Chance.
Title of Beatles' song

They make a wasteland and call it peace.

Calgacus, quoted by Tacitus

Now the hoes, the hard mattocks

and beaked plough share the

wealth of the countryside! Let

First keep the peace within yourself;

these shine, while weapons grow

then you can also bring peace to others.

dirty with mould. - **Ovid**

Thomas a Kempis

What is peace? Is it war? No. Is it strife? No.
It is lovely, and gentle, and beautiful;
and pleasant and serene and joyful.

Charles Dickens

onours to the world again

essed part to heaven, and slept

Nothing can bring you peace but yourself

Ralph Waldo Emerson

Lasting peace resides
not in extending the
ties of relationship
among princes by
marriage; nor in
treaties and alliances
which lead to wars...
Men must not be too
zealous about a
phantasm called
national glory, often
inconsistent with
individual happiness.

Erasmus

Peace – an idea whose time has co

Anatol Rapoport

Give peace in ou